Margaret Moore was born during the Second World War in 1942 in Leytonstone, East London. She left school at the age of 15, trained in secretarial skills and eventually obtained a much sought-after position of Legal Secretary in a London firm of solicitors – the start of a career which was to last for 37 years. Married with two sons and now two grandsons, she has spent most of her working life in Essex and Suffolk. Since her retirement in 2006 she has had a number of articles and interviews printed in the East Anglian press. Growing up as the second of four children in the 1940s and 50s, the family had little in terms of wealth but much in terms of laughter and imagination, a background which, she claims, has shaped and developed her sense of humour and given her a dedication to seeing the funny side of life.

SHORT POEMS FOR LITTLE PEOPLE

Margaret Moore

Book Guild Publishing
Sussex, England

First published in Great Britain in 2010 by
The Book Guild Ltd
Pavilion View
19 New Road
Brighton, BN1 1UF

Copyright © Margaret Moore 2010
Illustrations © Chris French

The right of Margaret Moore to be identified as the author of this work has been asserted by her in accordance with the Copyright, Designs and Patents Act 1988.

All rights reserved. No part of this publication may be reproduced, transmitted, or stored in a retrieval system, in any form or by any means, without permission in writing from the publisher, nor be otherwise circulated in any form of binding or cover other than that in which it is published and without a similar condition being imposed on the subsequent purchaser.

All characters in this publication are fictitious and any resemblance to real people, alive or dead, is purely coincidental.

Printed and bound in Thailand under the supervision of
MRM Graphics Ltd, Winslow, Bucks

A catalogue record for this book is available from
The British Library.

ISBN 978 1 84624 460 5

Thanks Mum and Dad for the legacy of laughter

Contents

Two Feet Tall	1
Granddad	2
Grandma	3
Where Are Baby's Teeth?	4
Questions	4
Grown-Ups	5
The Windy Day	6
Our Baby's Name	7
Is It A Long Way	8
The Stairs	8
The Journey	9
Raining	10
What Do Babies Do?	10
The New Arrival	11
An Aunty	12
New Shoes	12
My Little Sister	13
Learning	13
My Little Brother	14
Choices	15
Did I Do That?	15
The Telephone	16
In A Muddle	17
The Mouse	18
Red Slippers	19
Shopping	20
Where Is It?	20
While Mum's Away	21
Too High	22
The Grumbly Midge	23
The Mystery	23
Lost And Found	24
Granddad's Hair	25
Ten	26
My Tummy	26
The Surprise	27
Feeling Better Now	27
The Day Has A Friend	28
Feeling Poorly	29
Not Much Fun	30

My Pet	30
Who Is That?	31
My First Day	32
Waiting	32
Greens	33
So Cross	34
Bathtime	35
Bubbles	35
The Spider	36
Who Has Got It?	36
The Angry Boff	37
Full Up	38
The Odd Dog	38
Floating	39
Words	40
I Don't Think So	40
Catching	41
The Lost Shoe	41
Fighting	42
Hands And Feet	43
The Shoe Shop	43
What Have You Got?	44
Measles	44
Tripping Up	44
Thinking	45
Billy	46
Not A Good Day	46
Sink Or Swim	47
Trying and Tying	48
The Wellies	49
Socks and Shoes	50
Hiding	50
Oozle	51
The Birthday Party	52
The Umbly Bumbly	52
Who Can Fly?	53
The Hoover	54
Waiting To Grow	55
The Washing Machine	56
My Prayers	57

TWO FEET TALL

I see the World from two feet tall
Which isn't very tall at all.
I met a dog the other day
Who sees the World in the same way.

GRANDDAD

My granddad likes to sleep a lot
when he sits in his chair.
I wondered why that happened
every time that he sat there.

I looked around the back of it
and looked under the seat
But there was nothing to be seen
to make him go to sleep.

Perhaps when I am very old
when I'm at least fifteen,
I'll find out how the
snooze chair works
And what makes
granddad dream.

GRANDMA

Why do grandmas always do
Things like hugging and kissing you?
Why can't they be more like us
And say 'Hello' without a fuss?

WHERE ARE BABY'S TEETH?

I think our baby's lost her teeth
I can't see where they are.
Perhaps she does what granddad does
And keeps them in a jar.

QUESTIONS

I ask a lot of questions,
I always want to know,
I can be quite a nuisance,
Because they told me so.

If I don't ask these questions
I will never know.
I'll have to be a nuisance
But that's already so.

GROWN-UPS

Why do grown-ups always shout
the minute that you run about?
'Don't do that or you'll
fall over'
Is what they shout,
Because they're older.
I shout back 'Just you
wait and see'
But then fall down
and cut my knee.

THE WINDY DAY

I wanted to go out today
But was afraid I'd blow away.
They said the wind was very strong,
I couldn't see it – they must be wrong.

I stood outside the door to see.
The wind blew hard and frightened me.
I ran back in and shut the door.
I will stay in and play some more.

OUR BABY'S NAME

I thought I'd call our baby Zacharia Small,
Mum seemed to choose a lot of names
I didn't like at all.
She came home with our baby
All new and pink and small.
But when I took a closer look
She's not a Zak at all!

IS IT A LONG WAY?

How far is far away?
They never seem to say.
Is it past the corner shop?
Is that the place where I should stop?
I went right past the shop today.
It didn't seem too far away.

THE STAIRS

My sister climbed up on the stairs
And had a nasty tumble.
As she's so small and she can't speak
She couldn't even grumble.

THE JOURNEY

When we go out in the car
I always hope we don't go far.
I get fed up just sitting there
They point things out, I stare and stare.
But all I ask is 'Are we there?'

I sit, I fidget,
I moan and groan.
I do this until we get home.
They let me out, I run and shout.
I don't know why they take me out.

RAINING

Do you know where the rain comes from?
It comes out of the sky.
My dad says it's a nuisance,
And so I asked him why.

He said it always makes a mess
And he prefers it dry.
I don't think I have ever seen
Dry rain come from the sky.

WHAT DO BABIES DO?

Our baby doesn't seem quite right,
He sleeps all day and cries all night.
He doesn't use a knife and fork
He never plays and he can't walk.
I thought when I was told he'd come
That he would be a lot more fun.

THE NEW ARRIVAL

We've got a baby in the house,
I am as quiet as a mouse.
They hide him under lots of clothes,
All I can see is his small nose.

They say that he is going to be
Another handful, just like me.
I don't know what they mean at all.
My hands, I think, are still quite small.

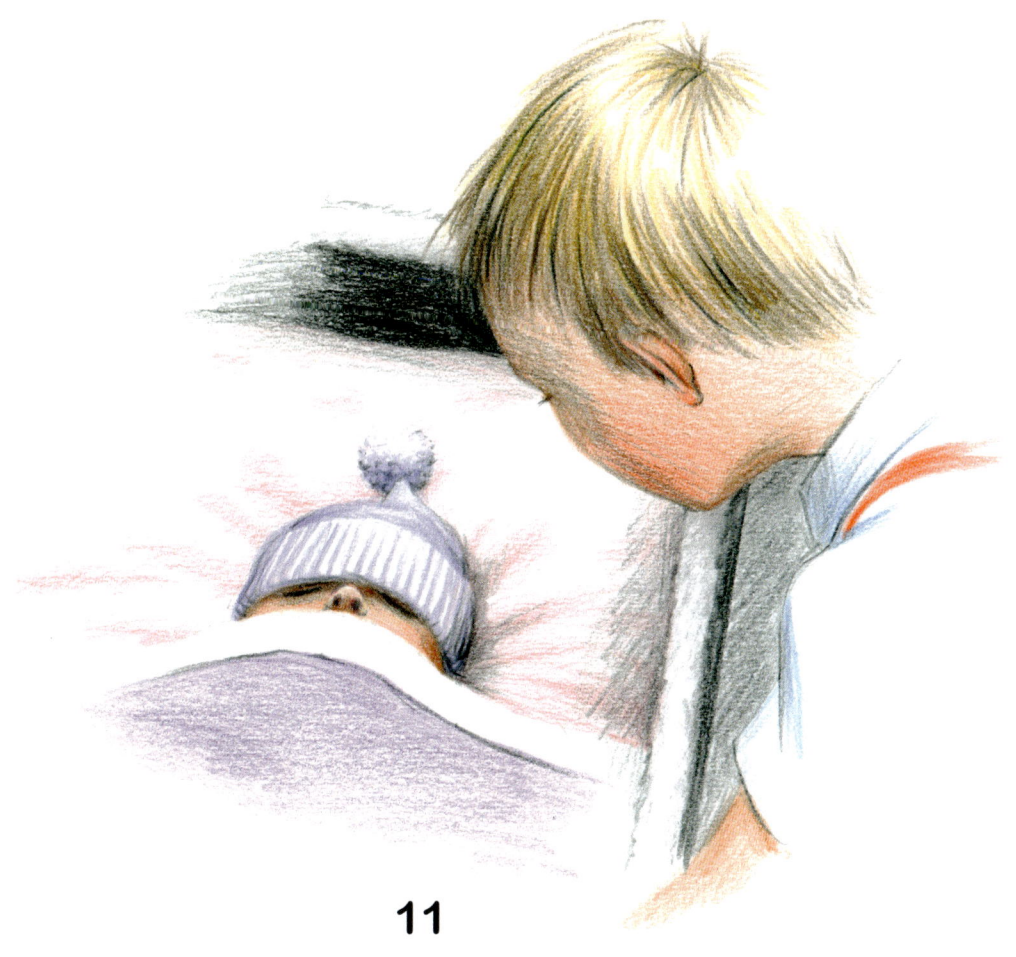

AN AUNTY

If you have an aunty,
I don't know what you get.
I'm told I've got an aunty
But I haven't seen it yet.
Is it something in a glass or is it in a box?
Whatever it turns out to be,
they tell me I've got lots.

NEW SHOES

My little sister wears no shoes,
She doesn't even talk.
She cries a bit and crawls around,
She doesn't even walk.
To choose new shoes you have to be
Nearly grown up just like me,
My little sister saw my shoes
I wonder if they're what she'd choose.
I can't tell if she likes my shoes,
but even so I told her
If she grows big and starts to walk,
She can have some when she's older.

MY LITTLE SISTER

I look after my sister as she is only three.
Because I am four, I know a lot more,
So she looks up to me.

When I look after my sister,
I have to open the door.
Because she can't reach the handle,
Until she's at least four.

LEARNING

When I was a baby, I had to learn to talk.
When I was a toddler, I had to learn to walk.
Now that I am three years old
I chat and run about,
But find that I am being told
'Sit still and do not shout'.

MY LITTLE BROTHER

With one foot going one way
And one foot going the other.
I laughed and watched the antics
Of my little brother.
He tried to do a cartwheel
and then he tried another.
I do enjoy the antics of my little brother.

CHOICES

Why can't I find just what I want?
It shouldn't be too hard
I only came into the shop
to pick a birthday card.

My friend is five years old you know
And he likes great big cards.
I can't find one I think he'll like,
it really is quite hard.

Perhaps I'll buy him sweets instead,
They've got some that I like.
I'm sure he'll like some sweets instead.
Yes, that sounds quite all right.

DID I DO THAT?

Our baby she does dreadful things,
She doesn't use her pot.
She doesn't tell us when she's been,
She does this quite a lot.
I don't think it is very nice.
The other day she did this twice!

THE TELEPHONE

The telephone rang, I thought I'd see
Who was trying to speak to me.
I picked it up and said 'Hello,'
There was a voice I did not know.
The voice said 'Just
who can that be?'
I said 'Oh! silly you,
it is me.'

IN A MUDDLE

Hats and coats are all right,
Gloves and shoes are fine,
But when I change
at School sometimes,
I wonder where are mine.

I nearly always
get it wrong
And come home in
a muddle.
I can't help it if I find
The whole thing too
much trouble.

THE MOUSE

I lost my mouse the other day,
I thought he had got clean away.
My sister went into her room,
There was a scream heard on the Moon.
I rushed into her room at speed
And told her there just was no need
To shout and scream and rant and rave
And popped him back into his cage.

RED SLIPPERS

I've got some new red slippers,
I keep them in their box,
I think they're rather special,
I like them lots and lots.

I haven't put them on yet,
I keep them on my bed,
I just like seeing my slippers,
All fluffy, new and red.

SHOPPING

We walk down to the bus stop,
We get up on the bus.
We do all of our shopping
without a lot of fuss.

But then I think that I am bored
And start to moan and groan,
Which means I get some sweeties
which last till I get home.

I know I shouldn't do it,
I know it is not right,
But that's what makes the shopping trip
More than just all right.

WHERE IS IT?

I know I saw it on the chair,
I've looked and looked just everywhere.
I'm trying to think where I have been,
It's been some time since we came in.
I don't think I can search some more,
I can't think what I'm looking for.

WHILE MUM'S AWAY

While mum was in hospital
dad took great care of me.
We had all sorts of strange things
for our dinner and our tea.
We had some chips and beans and things
And then we had some more.
I'm glad mum's back home again
with dinners as before.

TOO HIGH

Why is everything so big?
It really isn't fair,
To reach the cakes
And buns and things
I have to use a chair.

THE GRUMBLY MIDGE

I saw a Grumbly Midge.
He likes to raid our fridge.
Some days he eats and never stops.
I found him eating my ice pops.
I told him my dad says it's me.
He really must now let him see.
I'm not the one who's telling fibs.
There really is a Grumbly Midge.

THE MYSTERY

It's round and sort of fluffy.
It's big and sort of soft.
It's got three legs and rocks a bit.
I found it in our loft.

No one knows about it.
Goodness knows from where it's come.
I don't know what it's supposed to be.
But I think it's rather fun.

LOST AND FOUND

When I was two, I lost a shoe.
When I was three, I found it.
Now I am four, it fits no more.
So who cares now
about it?

GRANDDAD'S HAIR

'Where has granddad's hair gone?'
I asked my mum today.
She said he used to have a lot
But it has worn away.
I wonder if it is because
He wears a cap all day.
My friend he wears a cap at school
But his hair seems to stay.

TEN

Why do we have ten fingers?
Why do we have ten toes?
Why do we need so many?
I don't think anyone knows.

I try to use mine all at once
And always get in a muddle.
I think whoever invented me
Has caused me a lot of trouble.

MY TUMMY

I've got a big fat tummy,
They say it's too much food.
As that is what a tummy's for,
I think they're rather rude.

THE SURPRISE

I went to bed the other night
And all seemed quite OK
But when I woke my daddy said
'Just come and see what's in this bed.'
I peered and peered and I did see
A little sister, just like me.

My mummy said she came to us
Because she was just ready.
I went and got a gift for her,
I gave her my old teddy.

FEELING BETTER NOW

They said I was going to see grandma,
So I got dressed and in the car.
I hoped the journey would be quick,
But soon I started feeling sick.
I said I couldn't wait some more
And was quite sick upon the floor.

THE DAY HAS A FRIEND

Where does the day go when it ends?
I'm sure it must have lots of friends.
I like it when it's bright and warm.
I run and hide if there's a storm.

If rain comes down I sit and frown
Because my friends don't come around.
I think it has a friend called Moon
cos when it's gone, I find my room
Is bright and silver with its glow.
Oh! That's the place
where day must go.

FEELING POORLY

What is a cough?
It is not nice.
What is a cold?
It's sniffy.
What is the point of both of these?
You just feel tired
and squiffy.

NOT MUCH FUN

Learning to do things at school
Isn't very much fun at all.
They want me to learn how to write,
I said I wouldn't, but then I might.
To learn to read seems hard to do,
The words all seem a jumble too.
I'm four years old and I don't need
To learn to write or learn to read!

MY PET

I had a fish called Fred
But now that he is dead,
I have a cat called Ben,
So now I'm happy again.

WHO IS THAT?

I look into the mirror and what do I see?
A person who is dressed exactly like me.
I don't know how a mirror works,
I know it isn't magic.
I only know it works each time.
I think my mirror is rather fine.

MY FIRST DAY

I'm off to school, it's my first day.
If I don't like it, I won't stay.
My bag is packed, my coat is on.
I hope I won't be gone for long.

My mum says I must be quite brave.
I blow a kiss and give a wave.
I got as far as the front door
And found I worried more and more.
I cried a bit and, on the way,
Thought I'd stay at home today.

WAITING

To ride a bike you need to be
A bit older than just three,
So when I'm four I hope to say,
'Watch me while I race away'.

GREENS

I'm growing up fast they tell me,
I'm eating my meals each day.
But as fast as I eat my dinners,
The greens don't go away.

I'm doing my best to please them.
I even ate peas today.
My friend doesn't eat all his dinners,
And as far as I know he's OK.

SO CROSS

I was so cross I'd been told off
I thought I'd run away.
I packed my bag and strutted off
I thought I'd go that day.

I went straight down the garden path
But heard along the way,
There's cake for tea with buns and things.
I'll leave another day.

BATHTIME

I like to bath and splash about
The water makes me shout.
But just as I enjoy myself
It's time that I got out.

BUBBLES

There's nothing that can make me laugh
Quite like having a bubble bath.
The water froths and bubbles up
I scoop and pour it from a cup.
My face is pink and it would seem
It is the best way to get clean.

THE SPIDER

A spider ran across the floor
And hid beneath the kitchen door.
My brother he came with a cup
And tried to scoop the spider up.
We looked and searched without a sound,
The spider just could not be found.
I think his legs raced him away,
We'll probably see him another day.

WHO HAS GOT IT?

My uncle lost his temper,
I don't know where it is.
I heard him tell my aunty
She'd got him in a tizz.

I looked under the cushions
But could not find it there.
I don't know where his temper is,
Can't find it anywhere.

THE ANGRY BOFF

My teddy he needs mending,
His ear has been pulled off.
It wasn't me that did it,
It was an angry Boff.

An angry Boff is someone
Who breaks things when they're cross.
As I don't lose my temper,
It was the angry Boff.

FULL UP

We went to tea, my friend and me,
it was a special treat.
We'd been good boys and made no noise,
Our good had lasted all week.
We ate and ate, our cheeks were full,
We felt all big and round.
We ate so much that we both thought
Our tummies would hit the ground.
When we stood up, we rocked a bit,
We thought we would fall over.
We liked our tea, my friend and me
But are glad that it's all over.

THE ODD DOG

I know a dog who is very odd
He doesn't bark at all.
He climbs up trees just like a cat
And goes to sleep upon the mat.
I wonder how he got like that.

FLOATING

If I could float up in the air
I'd travel in a bubble,
But if some birds came too close by
I think I'd be in trouble.
They'd probably peck and poke at it
to see if it was food,
And as I'm quite a big boy now
I'd tell them they were rude.
A bubble doesn't last too long
and so it's best I stay,
Down on the ground
for some time yet and
fly another day.

WORDS

I've got a book with pictures in
And lots and lots of words.
As I can't read I think it is
Wonderfully absurd.

I DON'T THINK SO

It was time to go but I said 'No'
I really didn't want to.
Why do I have to stop my fun
Just as it has really begun?

CATCHING

My friend he sneezed and coughed a bit,
I thought it rather funny,
Until I found the next day that
my nose was rather runny.
I told my friend and he said
that if I had asked for more.
He would have passed his cold to me,
cos that's what friends are for.

THE LOST SHOE

I wonder what you have to do
if you're two and lost a shoe.
I had it on when we came out.
We've done some shopping and been about.

I don't know where my shoe has gone.
My mum asked 'Has it been gone long?'
I don't know what they're worried about.
I never walk when we are out!

FIGHTING

I got a smack, it wasn't right,
All I did was start the fight.
I didn't punch or kick at all,
I only pushed him so he'd fall.

His mother came and so did mine,
They asked a lot and then said,
'Fine, if you can't play without a row,
You'll both go home with us
        Right now'.

HANDS AND FEET

I have two hands, one left, one right,
I have two feet the same.
I don't know where they all came from,
They were with me when I came.

THE SHOE SHOP

I saw a shop full up with shoes.
I thought a shoe was hard to lose.
If all the shoes I saw were lost,
There are a lot of grown-ups, cross.

WHAT HAVE YOU GOT?

When I have a cold, they say I have a chill.
When I say I've had enough, they say
'Well, are you ill?'
If I have a little cough, they ask me why I did it.
I tell them I don't have a clue,
so off to bed I go, with flu!

MEASLES

Do you want my measles?
Do you want my spots?
You will have to bring a bag,
Because there are lots and lots.

TRIPPING UP

When I look down, I see my feet,
They stop me falling over.
Why is it then that when I'm out
They can be such a bother?

THINKING

What is a pet?
It can be anything you like.
A pet for me would have to be
Quite tough and quick and bright.
I think a dog, quite big and strong
Might be just right for me.
I'll have to think about it though
Because it's time
for tea.

BILLY

I have a friend no one can see,
He's always there and talks to me.
Some people say that I am silly
When I have chats with my friend Billy.

My mum says they don't really know
That my friend Billy will one day go
And when I'm older I will find
That my friend Billy was in my mind.

NOT A GOOD DAY

When I woke up I thought I'd be
Very good this morning.
But things went wrong
and so I found
By noon I'd had a warning.
By teatime I had had a smack
So that was quite the end of that.

SINK OR SWIM

My dad said I should learn to swim
So off we went and I plunged in.
I thought that I would, like a boat,
Have no trouble in staying afloat.

I found that I was sinking fast
I knew that this just couldn't last.
My dad he grabbed me by the shoulder,
Perhaps I'll swim when I am older.

TRYING AND TYING

I'm trying to tie a bow today,
I've tried to tie it in every way.
I twist it, I tie it, I pull it, I turn.
I simply can't do it.
I will never learn.

THE WELLIES

I have a pair of wellies,
They're big and new and green.
I put them on the other day
To walk in by the stream.
I thought I ought to try them out
And went to find a puddle.
I walked into a muddy mess
And now I am in trouble.

SOCKS AND SHOES

I know my shoes are dirty,
I know my socks look grey,
But when I take them off at night
They seem to fly away.
I stayed awake the other night
To see if I was right and,
Yes, I was, in came my mum
With fresh ones, nice and bright.

HIDING

I know that I am shy, but I don't know why.
I always want to hide away
When anybody comes to stay.
I find the best place here to hide
Is by dad's chair, so big and wide.
I might come out when they have gone.
I just hope they don't stay too long.

OOZLE

The Oozle Doozle bird flies very high,
He often has chats with the pilots who fly.
He is always careful to keep well away,
When an aircraft is cruising to your holiday.
But should you look out and see Oozle go by,
Please give him a wave
as he cruises on high.

THE BIRTHDAY PARTY

My birthday party was alright,
I even managed to have a fight.
One of the boys who came to it
Thought he'd be tough and barge a bit.
I told him he could not do that
And when he did, I struck him back.
We pulled and tugged upon the ground,
till finally my mum came round.
She stood us up and made us say
'Let's be friends and find a way
To play some games without a fight'
Then friends can visit another night.

THE UMBLY BUMBLY

The Umbly Bumbly is stupid and big.
He lives in a kennel but eats like a pig.
He doesn't wear shoes
and he doesn't use money.
He just loves to play
and roll on his tummy.

WHO CAN FLY?

I saw a bee go buzzing by.
I thought it must be fun to fly.
I stood upon the bathroom stool
And jumped and flapped
till I did fall.
No, flying is no fun at all.

THE HOOVER

My mum has got a big machine
That makes a lot of noise.
She keeps it in the cupboard
Away from little boys.
It has a lot of pipes and things
And also has a door.
A light comes on when she plugs in,
I asked her what it's for.
She told me it is to clear up
The mess that people make,
Especially when little boys
Eat lots and lots
of cake.

WAITING TO GROW

What can be the matter with me
I'd really like to know.
I eat my meals and stretch a lot
But simply do not grow.
My dad told me it is because
I'm in a great big hurry.
I'll grow a little bit
each day
And so I
shouldn't worry.

THE WASHING MACHINE

I looked into the window
and saw my socks go round,
There are a lot of bubbles
but they don't make a sound.
I caught glimpse of daddy's shirt
and also mummy's blouse,
When suddenly they all spun off
and left a sudsy cloud.
As I was wondering where they'd gone
they all appeared again,
but this time as they
Turned around
It seemed to
start to rain.
The water it came
tumbling down
And made them
wet again.

MY PRAYERS

I say my prayers most times at night
When I go up to bed.
I wonder if He'd mind if I
Save them for morning instead.